Cats Being Cunts

AN OFF COLOR- ADULT COLORING BOOK

Yes, it still looks like
bullshit
From down here too

Fluff Off

Your breathe smells
like tuna

I like it!

Fine
I'll feed
myself!

I do
what
I want

I PEED IN YOUR SHOES
SO YOU CAN THINK OF ME ALL DAY

DON'T JUDGE ~
I'VE SEEN THE
BITCHES
YOU'VE BROUGHT HOME!

Imma
Purrate

I LET MYSELF OUT
AND I THEN KILLED
THE GUY THAT PUT
ME IN IT

Right, I'm not "allowed"

on the table

Lesbians   Eat
WHAT?!

Best seat in the house?
You'll
need
to
move
the cat

Yes the cat has my tongue!

What do you call a cat who can get whatever it wants?

Purr~suasive

Just saving
the
goldfish

Where's
the
Partridge?

Love
CATS

Shuh Duh
Fuh Cup

FKUC
UOY

Scaredy

Cat

A NEW COUCH...
FOR ME ?!

Keep laughing
Only wet pussy
You've seen all week